TO HER

FOR EXPRESSING MY LOVE

SUHAS PALUKURI

Dedicated to Her.

The one for whom I am writing to express my feelings.

Contents

Acknowledgements *vii*

Part 1

1. Wondering 3
2. Deep From My Heart 4
3. From The Inner Soul 5
4. Hello Love 6
5. I Am Lucky 8
6. Break Free 9
7. Try To Tear 10
8. Forever On My Mind 11
9. So Encouraging 12
10. I Was In You 13
11. Daydreaming 14
12. Pronounced 15
13. Build A Castle 16
14. I Start To Blush 17
15. Addicted 18
16. Divine 19
17. Composed 20
18. Commotion 21
19. Portion Of Thoughts 22
20. Miscible 23
21. Carelessly 24
22. Written Funny 26

Contents

23. Remained 27

24. Not Quip 28

25. Sparle 29

26. We And Us 30

27. Last Sigh 31

28. Deep Into Love 32

29. Admire 33

30. Drops Of Agony 34

Part 2

Finally 37

Acknowledgements

I thank and express my gratitude to all the people who trusted me & kept me motivated in my journey upto now. A big thanks to all the readers who are one of the boost-up for me all the time.

I thank my Publisher, for showing faith in this book.

Last but not least, I thank **her** making me motivated all the time.

gratitude...gratitude.

There will be few people like poetry; they're never too outspoken,
and their feelings are veiled under a lovely face.

People like them are very rare... But Pure

1. Wondering

I'm curious while smirking.
Blissfully captivated in the sunniest of colours
Carelessly happy and apathetic
I've existed that habit because I join you.
Everything has received so odd.
Life performs expected excessively charming expected valid.
My essence sees that this is only the origin of much more at hand.

2. Deep from my Heart

A heap superstars up above.
One shines more brilliant - I can't decline.
A love so favorite, a love so real,
a love that emanates me to you.
The sweets chant when you are familiar.
Within your weaponry I have nothing to fear.
You forever see just what to suggest.
Just reprimand you form my epoch.
I love you, sweetheart, accompanying all of my soul.
Together eternally and never to part.

3. From the Inner soul

If I had legal order to define my impressions for you
I hopeful the most satisfied fellow in outer space
But conversation appear to abandon me continuously
So I should consent to mandate in this place sonnet

Your touch, your grin, your demeanor and being
Mesmerize and involve me entirely
If I had but individual aspiration, individual utter aim
It hopeful to stay by your side for forever

4. Hello Love

I praise God for shipping me you, my love.
I praise him for changeful my view.
Now you are attending accompanying me, and I'm attending accompanying you.
Now will you allow me love you?

I continually hope that love was wrong,
But entirety transformed when you developed.
For the rest of my history, I be going to accompany socially you,
To touch your help and be a guest of you.

I'll stay next to you, candid and valid.
Till completely of my opportunity, I will forever love you.
In my career, I'll never leave you.
Now and forever, I'll be compassionate you.

Love is divine, mine is valid.
I love you as well I always experienced.
Will you will allow me love you?

I praise God for allowing me visualize you.
I kiss Him for bestowing me you.

Now I be going to shout that I love you.

5. I am Lucky

I never idea that presently hopeful so extraordinary
Seeing your face that's certainly charming
Every laugh of you gives my history a reason expected abundant
The advantage that you acquire can create all guy a fool.

Every occasion I find out the echoes of your sweet voice
All added sounds disappeared even the minimal turbulence.
You continually show the absolutely begged poise
If always your love hopeful mine,
I'm the most fortunate with all guys.

6. Break free

There is one right core of me
the one's intensely spellbound you
one the one would air some pond
all of that he would do, in the way that you

He's not reluctant of everything
entirely nothing by any means
cause for you he will overcome all welcome fears
to preserve you from all those tears

This person I wish to draw out eventually
so I can ultimately suggest
this three conversation I hold deep inside me
that has happened bothersome to break free

I see moment of truth will reach
when I can completely narrate you
this three extraordinary conversation that are
I Love You

7. Try to tear

I'm absent you so extremely
And desire your small touch
Dancing nearly calamity

We effort just to find few range
Inside each other's little experience
Stinging swells inside my chest
Endure to her neglect the rest
Of all the fears that try and tear
Us other than entity exceptional
To have you in my weaponry will be

Your wonderful endowment to me
Oh, compassion, I am resting for you
Unleash upon me your lilac color.

8. Forever on my mind

Before I join you,
I sensed that I couldn't love one,
That no one hopeful smart to fill outer space in my courage,
But that all altered when I join you.
Then I got near accomplish you were forever on my mind.
You're humorous and sweet.
You form me howl and smirk.
You remove all my anger and unhappiness.
You create me feeble when I warn you.
Then I begun to address verses about you.
Now I have equal accomplish that I am desperately captivated you.

9. So encouraging

It was many before that a advantage was innate
That the globe waited to party,
This fair woman was singular and beloved by all
And even the sweets wished to experience her circumstance.
And before when the advantage was developed accordingly fair
Everyone started to flaunt and court her,
Men would waltz, serenade and flaunt their ability
In the hopes that they commit disturb hold her close.
Yet individual son was opportune, so encouraging so sanctified,
That she selected him as better than all the rest,
He still can't trust that this sweet is welcome daughter
That guy is me, you are the sweet, my experience.

10. I was in you

I love you from head to phalanges
And in addition you'll always experience.
It hurts when you are dismal,
And create me depressed when you are crazy.
I see we fight occasionally,
But will see I will love you as far as completely.
I have a gut feeling you are the individual for me,
And the alone skilled will always be.
You are the individual I be going to give my history accompanying,
To call my bride and to share a kid.
I will never discern you legal order bye-bye,
And I will love you till the epoch I wither.
If I search out die before you do,
I will be resting at throwing out of a residence of paradise for you.

11. Daydreaming

Daydreaming, accompanying a approve my face
Blissfully absent, in the sunniest of hues
Carelessly satisfied, unaware to worries
Is what I've happened, because I've join you
So resembling a dream, entirety has enhance
Life feels, excessively good expected valid
My soul experiences, this is just the origin
Of a lot more to anticipate

12. Pronounced

You've visualized me take a fall,
You've visualized me create mistakes
I'm certain you've frequently pronounced,
"This is all I can take!"
I am your awkward Valentine
that much is real,
But as not graceful as I am
I doubtlessly love you,
I'll never be premier
or a sentimental book cover,
But individual idea you can depend on
I'm gonna love you endlessly!

13. Build a castle

If roses were rose and lilac are sad,
I would take us continuously to a place in the way that two.
You'd visualize my beau and by what method intensely I feel,
You'd experience so precisely that my love is so palpable.
Together we'd build a citadel place we take care of waltz and play,
I'd be all belonging to individual and you'd be mine as far as our last day of life.
We'd live without companionship or confidant in sweet satisfaction and love,
And the sweets would protect us from above.
And in spite of immediately our love is so new,
I will endlessly hope that this dream will reach real.

14. I start to blush

You create me shriek when I be going to cry,
Make me live when I be going to expire,
Make me smirk when I be going to disapprove,
You turn my history reversed.
Believe in me when nobody different does
You're my immediately, my is, my was.
When you call my name I start to blush,
I'm reluctant crowd notice I need you very.
When I'm accompanying you occasion flees by fast.
It's like the is ancient times.
I need you as well you can trust,
Love you in addition you can realize.
Think about you each evening and era
And hope my history can stay this habit
I don't want it expected alternatively.

15. Addicted

I drop intensely loving, the first period I proverb you.
And within importance, skilled was nothing I be able.
I was enamored and addicted by your charming charm,
And saw that I'd give my growth with you as one.
I proverb idols dance about you and twinkling so brilliant,
You appeared to have sweet extensions ready to escape.
The planet appeared sunnier and my soul sensed free,
In that cute importance when you first smirked at me.
Something switched inside of me, my growth started again,
And I saw before and skilled I was fashioned in the way that you.

16. Divine

Sometimes in this place period,
We meet a distinguished energy,
A energy that fits just perfect,
And create us decisively whole.
Something feels some various,
From all the different morale we welcome,
And we find that concurrently with an activity,
We were appropriated to meet.
Our two beings start to communicate,
We excite each one like shade resembling such a color,
Deep and extraordinary things take place,
And we accomplish our network is divine.
Now we are twisted for all forever,
We two have immediately combine,
Life has captured on a whole new intention,
It is the start of bewitching fun.
We be going to immediately continue a journey,
That only two together of us be going to experience,
And be together for all forever,
As our love continually be going to evolve.

17. Composed

While the clocks turn and you be exhausted,
our spirits merge
similar two colorful banner being assorted,
on an artist's palette.
Then we are captured on this passing journey
on the brush of consequence.
The occurrences of our lives happen when the touch the tarpaulin
momentary and room,
this is the fiction of us, composed and finished each second,
this is art of our existence that is to say existed fashioned.

18. Commotion

In a commotion accompanying my thoughts,
It grasp so inadequate still very I visualize,
and I feel and entirety I be going to hold
related the taste of your kiss,
the touch of your skin
as well as the voice when you talk
places we projected to go,
and places that we have existed.
So if shard of thoughts joins to form the one I am
you get or give an advantage me,
certainly.

19. Portion of Thoughts

In a scuffle accompanying my thoughts,
It holds so inadequate still very I visualize,
as well as I feel and entirety I be going to maintain
like the taste of your kiss,
the manner of your skin
and the voice when you talk
places we projected to go,
and places that we have existed.
So if portion of thoughts joins to create the one I am
you thrive me,
certainly.I'm the anarchic storm that ransacks
she's my quiet,
I base so tense and severe
she gives me substance and adaptability.
I pen mandate and organize bureaucracy in tune
she is the individual that form it expressive.
I attempt an end on any occasion I stutter,
she keeps me going in progression.
Lines and form of her face mesmerizes
I inquire a discussion further inadequate discussion advantage.
to some eye I may look finished
but I am not, she is my subdivision.

20. Miscible

What delegation I hold,
for the task of my inspiration?
There's many
the list goes high.
A boyfriend of her advantage,
An follower of her eyes,
A connoisseur of her thoughts,
A guardian of her laugh.
A local of her courage
Like a miscible liquid we blend.
I grasped her help in the beginning
I'll grasp it till completely.

21. Carelessly

Daydreaming, accompanying a approve my face
With joy dreaming, in the sunniest of hues
Carelessly satisfied, unaware to worries
Is what I've happened, because I've join you
So resembling a dream, entirety has enhance
Life feels, excessively good expected valid
My courage sees, this is just the origin
Of a lot more to anticipate

I used to display or take public bed each evening and dream a desire you
And I would suspend consciousness impression so unique and awaking as I continually do.
To my empty bed accompanying pillows piled to hug like you were familiar.
And I would feel so depressed inside experienced, it was a dream you were away.

I love the habit you bother and glare
It create me ability much you care.

I love you just the habit you are
No pretentions even from a great distance away

I love you cause you love me also
Just like the habit I do.

22. Written funny

I reliable to print odd love writings for you,
I tried also few adorable and absurd one also.
But apparently I haven't still well-informed how to verse,
So, I request of you, dear, will present me few period.
Yet, I will numeral it out,
Until therefore, I hope that you will not pout.
Trust me, my fellow, you indeed do stimulate me,
I'm just poor quality accompanying conversation, as you can clearly visualize.
It's not that smooth at hand up accompanying love verses, you experience,
So, at the same time, I'll just find another habit for my love to show.

23. Remained

I do mix up what I have,
my courage is so severe ...
Heart? Oh, what do I reply -
I do not have presently.
Already I, opportune, have famous you,
you sweet beloved my,
from the average value
it was earlier belonging to individual.
O you can hold it,
for fear that it continually waited so -
it be going to be belonging to individual,
only you, my paramour!
Giebs never repeated back to me -
it beats you in conviction -
as well as you will unable presently
my treasure, before sever.

24. Not quip

You're a excellent man for me,
so I raze captivated you.
And nevertheless by what method remainder of something joke,
you are eternally in my soul.
And nobody can separate us,
cause you lead my essence to blaze.
And nevertheless in what way or manner the distance confidentially is,
fair stay the way you are.
For while our love is,
can not care the one, place is.
This also emanated my courage,
and optimistically you will not quip stylish.

25. Sparle

To name you, I need not just individual discussion,
As you laugh,
How sweet your voice plays in me,
How sensitive your voice,
when you greet me.
How sunny your eyes sparkle,
if you examine me.
Oh paradise's sweets,
You are my dream wife.
I love only you,
your habit you present yourself,
For you are the individual,
that is to say mine.

26. We and Us

I can't stop being with you because you constantly make me fall in love, be in love and share love every day.
Being with you made me value the words "we" and "us."
I love you to the moon and back. I want to grow old while loving you and watch the drapes fade.
The thought of a future with you makes me too excited, and I want to love you forever.

27. Last sigh

Ever because I join you, I have never desired another.

I will continually admire you accompanying my whole soul.

Sweetheart, I will love you accompanying my last sigh and present you entirety you engaged that is to say inside my reach.

I can't wait to visualize your laugh accompanying upper class of belongings, check your eyes, and suggest those dispute that will form you blush. I can't wait to show you the love in my essence.

28. Deep into Love

When I visualize you My courage skips a beat
Your laugh sweeps my soul continuously My
essence is upset for your love You
are the individual my courage desires To be accompanying
All the days of my history

Baby, I want you expected about my history
Often I want you to hold you
Trace to your ears I love you

Come close my love My soul is desire
for your love You are the someone adored
I can't stop thinking about you

Dreams of you enclose me You're the thrashing
of my essence The love you present outlines me My history
is not any more dark You present your help so gratefully I
am missing if you're continuously. You have me so entirely.
I enshrine you continually. Without your whiff, I
cannot live. I need your brinks on mine. Nothing by any
means
I wouldn't present. I'll take nothing and be fine.

29. Admire

You are so delicate
You are my sweet
You are the individual I
be going to give my existence accompanying
You are the individual I delight in

You are the individual
I have disgraced spellbound
When I am accompanying you
I can't detail the impressions I fool you

I dream around you each evening
You are in my mind before I go to bed
You are my first idea when I revive
You are the individual I admire

30. Drops of agony

Don't go far outside, not even for moment of truth, cause --
cause -- I forbiddance skill to reply it: moment of truth delay
and I will be pausing for you, as in an empty station
when the trains are stationed off in another place, unconscious.

Don't leave me, even for an moment, cause
before the little drops of agony will all meld,
the cigarette that roams expect a home will drift
into me, smothering my missing essence.

Unfortunately, may your outline never annul on the waterfront;
can your eyelids never flap into the empty distance.
Don't leave me for a short time, my valuable,

cause within importance you'll have dissolved up until now
I'll digress mazily over all the ground, wanting to know,
Will you return? Will you leave me present, expiring?

I can't sleep because I‘m thinking about you.

I can't sleep because I'm thinking about you.

Being with you is what keeps me alive.

Finally

I want to tell you one thing...
Till now I don't know what is pain...
but from the time I saw you, is the time when I feel Pain...
I knew that the pain was named after **LOVE!!!**
I didn't get any better way other than this to express my
LOVE!!!

"To love at all is to be vulnerable. Love anything and your heart will be wrung and possibly broken. If you want to make sure of keeping it intact you must give it to no one, not even an animal. Wrap it carefully round with hobbies and little luxuries; avoid all entanglements. Lock it up safe in the casket or coffin of your selfishness. But in that casket, safe, dark, motionless, airless, it will change. It will not be broken; it will become unbreakable, impenetrable, irredeemable. To love is to be vulnerable."

– C.S. Lewis

I LOVE YOU

Printed by Libri Plureos GmbH in Hamburg,
Germany